New Beginnings

Stephanie Jarema

ISBN: 978-93-6354-744-5

First Edition: 2026
Rs. 200/-

Cyberwit.net
HIG 45 Kaushambi Kunj, Kalindipuram
Allahabad - 211011 (U.P.) India
http://www.cyberwit.net
Tel: +(91) 9415091004
E-mail: info@cyberwit.net

Printed at Repro India Limited.

Contents

No More

Screaming, crying
All alone in this world.
Anxious, unhappy
Separated
Goodbye

Hold On

Hold on it's been one hell of a ride
Hold on, let go of the fears inside.
Hold on, it's been quite a year.
Wishing and thanking the universe for a new change.
Hold on it's been a wild ride,
My anxiety has left me, now I'm free to go on with my life.
Hold on,
I'm still figuring out my life.
It's not over but just beginning to feel just right
And I'm coming out on the other side.

Sunshine

You are a breath of fresh air on a hot summer day
You take my anxiety and nerves away
You are my warmth on a cold winters' day
You warm me up and bring sunshine on a dull cloudy day
You are my sun when it pours rain
You take my sadness and sorrows away
You are my light and warmth on any given day
You light me up and make me feel safe
I miss you and hate to say goodbye
But I'll see you soon again my love
I hope these moments never end
My partner and best friend.

The Scars

The scars are deep as they never fade
I am still healing from all the hurt and pain
The scars are deep as you left me anxious and afraid
Will this feeling of doubt ever go away?
The scars are deep as I keep moving forward
and leave the past behind
You were never there for me, but I left without looking back
The scars are deeper as I will never return to the place
Where I am not enough.
I am strong and will keep pushing through
Until I find someone who doesn't
Leave the scars so deep but helps them fade away
Into the past I left behind.

Told

I was told you can' t be yourself, but I did
I was told what to do but I ignored you and found my own way
I was told you're not smart enough, but I proved them wrong
I was told you are not good enough, but I came back stronger than ever before
You told me I couldn't see or talk to my friends, but I did it anyway!
You told me I'd never be able to be on my own,
But I am now and enjoying life without being told, without your control
I told you!

You

You left me the breadcrumbs
While I stayed by your side.
Now I'm moving on to find someone
Who will be worthy of my love.

Goodbye

I left you behind showed me the good bad and the ugly
Love bombing
Gaslighting
Blame
Shame
Goodbye

Dreamy Night

I met you in my dreams last night as I looked towards your way.
I met you in my dream last night and you lifted my pain away.
I met you in my dreams last night when we kissed for the first time.
I met you in my dreams last night, where we fell in love underneath the stars.
I met you in my dreams last night and woke up with you beside me in real life.

The Space Between Us

The space between us keeps me quiet here.
The space between us fills an empty space,
As I stand alone quietly to only remember the sad look on your face.
The space in between us keeps me quiet here,
I'm lost without you but not afraid of fear.
The space in between us fills an empty space,
For it is hard to forget a familiar face.
The space between us, leave me coming back for more,
For it is only you that I truly adore.
Don't look back now but I've found someone new,
For the space between use doesn't exist anymore.
The space between us is erased as I move on without you,
and there is no more empty pain.

Someone to Hold

I want someone to love,
Someone to hold,
Someone to keep me safe and warm
Someone to keep me young and grow with old.
I want to find someone soon
Maybe that someone could be you.

Tattered and Torn

My love between the sheets are all tattered and torn
You said you love me, but left me here alone.
Without any warning, without any fuss,
You never really fought for us.
My heart is torn, and I really did love you.
Now my thoughts of you are a distant memory,
You broke my heart, and I will always have you on my mind,
There is no more love to share now that it is all tattered and torn.

Silence

Sitting in silence with my thoughts while no one is here to listen.
Sitting in silence as I have found my inner strength and peace.
Sitting in silence where nothing is out of reach.
There is nothing left to lose and so much to gain while I get over the pain.
Sitting in silence, I can breathe again.
I can breathe again.
Sitting in silence, I don't feel any more pain.
I just feel the left-over memories that are so far away.
Sitting in silence I can breathe again
Sitting in silence, I found my inner strength.
Sitting in silence,
I've found peace and I can move on and just breathe.

Truth Telling

Why can't I pronounce my love for you?
For it secretly grows though morning
as summer blossoms consume after day.
Only dark wild winds will sound
if these minutes of truth telling shower away.

Arise

Hot summer days and cool crisp nights,
As I lay down beside you and hold you tight.
There is no worry,
There is no fear as long as I have you nearby.
Bright stars in the dark night sky,
As I lay down beside you and watch shooting stars fly by.
There is no rush; only time stands still as we sit here and chill.
Morning sunlight and clear blue skies,
As I lay awake beside you and arise.

Slender Lace

I want you for wild red love as minutes grow full consuming all of you.
Put off evening work as wind sounds though crack tendril glass.
We have immense mornings by day, yet it is dark after we run away.
All to see skin and slender lace.

Endless Days

When will my love be found?
After wild wind shoers dry out,
I am growing red over blue songs.
As the slender cracks consume
Page secrets away from morning,
Yet to tell and ask him for endless days.

Ghost

I tell you to leave after minutes of dark immense showers,
Blue songs dry out.
Let the wind grow wild as glass cracks slender away from sounds.
You secretly stagger over red bruises consumed.
What did I teach you?
Run off, go see about days without asking about me and you.

With You

Happy Lonesome
Down and Blue
Bright clear skies appear when I'm with you.

Fully Tongued

I will only love you if blossoms grow wildly
Smelling dry winds as dirt cracks through skin as lace.
Stagger away with blue songs
Consuming dark secrets by day.
Put off these minutes and leave fully tongued.

Half Full

Empty pages are waiting to be filled,
As my thoughts unfold.
It's long overdue to be writing again,
And see myself through these empty pages
and thoughts half full.

Life as a Book

Life is like a book as chapters unfold,
Retelling memories of new and old.
Life as an apple to cut and slice,
Picking up seeds and letting them grow.
Life as a blanket so warm but limb,
I never know just how many people
can be so cold and grim.
Life as a light bulb so bright and dim,
A flick of a switch and that could be it.
Life as a book tattered and torn,
As pages go missing to find a new chapter
and purpose rather than worn.

Lips

Delicate and sweet
Wet and dry
Caressing love
A kiss.

Secret in Song

The red morning blossoms are here!
Wild skin bruised as slender showers sound away.
You stagger about yet minutes are up.
Will I not see these days grow?
Leave my secret in song,
As I run over to Avenue Road
To tell you, we are in love.

Summer

I immensely consume passion, love, and desire.
Life will let us grow and build these pages from morning to night.
Let summer arrive soon as we stagger away.
Come celebrate and whisper like wild bouquets.
Put off minutes too late and run by the sounding wind
and do not ask me why.
Let's go and leave right away and let summer begin.

Long Forgotten

Long Forgotten are the days when we were a pair,
As I loved you and truly cared.
Long forgotten unspoken words meant to say
Before I left you and you expected me to stay.
Long forgotten love songs written about you.
For now, they no longer exist.
Long forgotten feelings of hurt and pain
As you leave me here and say, "I'm sorry."
I walked away
I walked away
After those long-forgotten words and thoughts of you disappeared.
As I move forward, I will find someone new.
I'm doing fine without you.
I've found someone new.

Mine

My hands for holding you
My arms for hugging you so tight
I don't want to let go but hold you all night.
My lips kiss you so softly and passionately.
I miss you and it comes so naturally.
My eyes to see that I've found you
and my heart is ready to love you and call you mine.

Faded

Why are you still here after I left you behind?
The memories of you have faded
And there is nothing more to say.
Leave the past behind, of you, us and I.

Wondering

Searching, Wondering
Find true destiny
Soulful, freedom
Dreamer

New Life, New Day

New life, new day
as everything changes,
And old memories fade to shades of grey.
Time is moving forward to start
and begin something wonderful,
All to find a new life and new day.

Adored

Gratitude, Happiness
Lost but now found
Timeless, Endless
Love

Forever and Hide

Why is this not over yet?
A song burns wild blue
for we can get through this
Dark bruises will heal
Let's go away after morning
where I can grow there only with you
Tell me about summer,
like blossoming shower bouquets
When I stagger out secretly
what is it like for you?
Consume and teach me to love you fully
with the immense sound and smells burning up inside
Put off the evening showers
so we can ride away together
forever and hide.

Full

I love growing with you
These mornings consume immense songs by day
and wild smells at an evening meal.
There you secretly leave,
minutes after the wind shower.
We are full.

www.ingramcontent.com/pod-product-compliance
Ingram Content Group UK Ltd.
Pitfield, Milton Keynes, MK11 3LW, UK
UKHW041317190726
13845UKWH00025B/322

9 789363 547445